Kassandra Castillo

The Causes That Lead Teenagers to Drug and Alcohol Abuse

GRIN - Verlag für akademische Texte

Der GRIN Verlag mit Sitz in München hat sich seit der Gründung im Jahr 1998 auf die Veröffentlichung akademischer Texte spezialisiert.

Die Verlagswebseite www.grin.com ist für Studenten, Hochschullehrer und andere Akademiker die ideale Plattform, ihre Fachtexte, Studienarbeiten, Abschlussarbeiten oder Dissertationen einem breiten Publikum zu präsentieren.

Dokument Nr. V125033 aus dem GRIN Verlagsprogramm

Kassandra Castillo

The Causes That Lead Teenagers to Drug and Alcohol Abuse

GRIN Verlag

Bibliografische Information der Deutschen Nationalbibliothek: Die Deutsche Bibliothek
verzeichnet diese Publikation in der Deutschen Nationalbibliografie; detaillierte bibliografische Daten sind im Internet über http://dnb.d-nb.de/ abrufbar.

1. Auflage 2008
Copyright © 2008 GRIN Verlag
http://www.grin.com/
Druck und Bindung: Books on Demand GmbH, Norderstedt Germany
ISBN 978-3-640-30490-5

Running Head: Causes That Lead Teenagers to Drug

The Causes That Lead Teenagers to Drug and Alcohol Abuse

Outline of the Paper

The Causes That Lead Teenagers to Drug and Alcohol Abuse

I. Introduction

A. Opening Statements

The family is the basic unit of society. Families are composed of parents and their children who live in a community. In the case of the United States of America, there are myriad challenges to families that affect teenagers. The common problems that beset teenagers are drug abuse, alcohol abuse, sexual molestation and teenage pregnancy. Research findings state that in the year 2008, 35.6% of students had had six or more drinks of alcoholic beverages on at least one occasion (Dew, 2009, p. 1). In addition, 70% of eleventh grade students have had at least one drink of alcoholic beverages during their lifetime through the influence of friends and family members (Dew, 2009, p. 1). Hence, the problem of alcohol abuse has escalated through the years.

The problem on drug abuse has increased through the years since according to the National Survey on Drug Use and Health, there were 9.5% of teenagers aged 12 to 17 who are currently drug users nowadays (Aldworth et. al., 2007, p. 45). These problems are results of the weakening of family values and ethical standards which make teenagers deviate from the norms. In other words, drug abuse, alcohol abuse, sexual molestation, commission of crimes and teenage pregnancy create challenges for families.

B. Thesis statement

The problems of teenagers involving drug abuse and alcohol abuse are primarily caused by stressful life events, peer influence, and failure of parents to take their children away from harmful activities. Besides, drug abuse and alcohol abuse might lead to sexual abuse or molestation and teenage pregnancy as well as the commission of violent crimes.

C. Importance of topic

The need to solve social problems like drug abuse and alcohol abuse makes it imperative to study the cases that lead teenagers to deviate the norms in society. The knowledge taken from the research paper is also useful in framing correct solutions for the problem.

Who has written about the subject (who has informed your paper):

Dinkmeyer (1990), McKay, De Guzman (1990) and Temke (2006) are authors that have written about the influence of parents on their children. Hobbs (2008) and Pasch (2003) are authors that have written about peer influence and peer pressure on teenagers. Regoli (2000), Wattenberg (2003), Henderson (2008) and Hendrickson (2001) are other authors that have informed this research paper.

D. Road Map

The cases that lead teenagers to drug and alcohol abuse include stressful events, peer influence, and failure of parents to keep their children away from harmful activities. This paper will discuss the reasons why teenagers become victims of drug and alcohol abuse which might cause sexual abuse or molestation against them, and teenage pregnancy despite the presence of their respective families and attendance in formal schools. After that, a discussion on the linkage of teenage drug and alcohol abuse with the commission of violent crimes will be given. It will also discuss the course of action for the treatment and intervention of teenagers who have fallen prey to drugs and excessive intake of alcoholic beverages as solution to the problem.

II. The Cases That Lead Teenagers to Drug Abuse and Alcohol Abuse

The primary cases that lead teenagers to drug abuse and alcohol abuse include stressful life events, peer influence, and failure of parents to take their children away from harmful activities.

A. Stressful Events

Stressful events in life cause trouble to teenager who attends school or not. Stressful life events may include divorce or separation of parents, low grades in school, and poverty. Divorce or separation of parents can affect the emotional, psychological, and physical well-being of a child. The primary concern of parents who are divorcing is the response of their children and their ability to handle the situation to become healthy and happy despite the problem (Temke, 2006, p. 1).

It must be remembered that the effects of divorce on children depends upon their age and gender. In this case, adolescents feel anger, depression, guilt, fear and

loneliness due to divorce of their parents (Temke, 2006, p. 2). Other teenagers are forced to hold mature responsibilities like taking care of their siblings and or earning a living for the broken family. The pressure of choosing one parent over the other is also stressful for a teenager.

Teenagers are irreparably damaged due to divorce of their parents. The situation makes teenagers think that they are too powerless to handle such family change. Family relationships are affected by the decision of parents to opt for divorce instead of saving the marriage which makes children feel guilty and depressed. Drug and alcohol abuse is often the means of coping for teenagers to ease the pain of having a broken family.

Moreover, the most common effect of divorcing parents is the inability of teenagers to cope with the changes in their family (Temke, 2006, p. 2). As a result, teenagers react negatively on the situation by resorting to drugs or alcoholic beverages. Hence, parents who are divorcing must help their children to adjust to the situation through proper communication and unconditional love and care. Divorcing parents must not neglect their children despite existing change in family setting. When their children grow up and become teenagers, the social stigma of living with a broken family will haunt them and make them walk astray.

Another stressful event in the life of a teenager is having low grades in school. Although this problem is related to lack of confidence, parents must not take it for granted. Studies mentioned that working memory deficits of a teenager may trigger some learning difficulties and behavioral troubles linked to impulsivity, difficulties in focus, and hyperactivity (⬚Working memory, psychiatric symptoms, and academic performance at school⬚). Depression may also cause low performance of teenagers in school. It is also considered the gateway of resorting to drugs and alcohol abuse.

Teenagers who got low grades in school can resort to drug abuse and alcohol abuse in order to ease their pain due to low morale and lack of self-confidence. Drug use is viewed as deriving from failing to make good in school activities and assignments (Regoli & Hewitt, 2000, p. 268). In short, some teenagers who are unable to gain success in academic matters may choose deviant modes of adaptation to deal with their failure.

In addition, poverty may also cause stress to teenagers. Logically, inability of parents to provide enough resources for the physical and financial needs of a teenager is unacceptable but existing today. Some teenagers are forced to be exposed to

environmental toxins and family violence, suffer instability of residence, and fewer learning experiences due to poverty (Gunn & Duncan, 1997, p. 2). Others are forced to work while studying just to make both ends meet. Due to lack of proper education, teenagers who belong to poor families experience difficulty in making themselves financially stable. As a result, some teenagers are involved in illegal activities like drug pushing which makes them mingle with people who are considered bad influence for them (Gunn & Duncan, 1997, p. 2). If teenagers are exposed to illegal activities, resorting to alcohol abuse and drug abuse cannot be avoided. Therefore, stressful events like poverty, divorce, and lack of proper education must be abated or lessened in order to prevent teenagers from resorting to drug abuse and alcohol abuse.

B. Peer Influence

One of the reasons why teenagers behave in a deviant manner is peer influence. Despite the earnest guidance of parents, some teenagers may still walk astray by means succumbing into pressure and influence (□Peer Influence on Deviant Behavior□). The reason of the existence of peer influence is the will of a teenager to make friends with other people. It cannot be denied that friendships are vital to the life of teenagers. Friendships among teenagers are essential factor of development. They give secure venues where teenagers can discover their identities, where they experience being accepted and where they can expand a sense of belongingness (de Guzman, 2007, p. 1). Besides, friendships among adolescents permit them to practice and cultivate social skills relevant for future success.

Peer influence among teenage friendships may either be positive or negative. The problem starts to breed when a teenager is a victim of negative peer pressure in the society. Parents worry for their teenagers who might neglect family values and beliefs due to negative peer influence. Other teenagers are also pressured to involve themselves with high-risk activities and other unacceptable behaviors and attitudes. Actual situations prove that peer influence is more complex than engagement with negative influence with friends.

The rationale behind the statement is the fact that peers had long been pointed as important element in the initiation and continuous use of drugs and alcohol (Pasch, 2003, p. 1). Several teenagers experienced peer pressure in relation to hobbies, interests, and entertainment. Friends of a teenager who drink alcoholic beverages and abuse drugs

may influence the latter to do the same. There is difficulty to stay away from peer pressure because friendships that occur during adolescent period are more consistent, exclusive and intimate (de Guzman, 2007, p. 1). Hence, teenagers must see to it that their friends would not encourage them to use drugs and drink alcohol.

In connection, there are effective strategies in avoiding and coping with peer influence. Peer influence may not be necessarily negative, but it can surely lead teenagers towards deviant behaviors. In order to lessen the effects of peer pressure against teenagers, there is a need for parents, youth, academic community, and government leaders to work together and establish effective strategies for that purpose. Parents must support the transition of their children from adolescence to mature adulthood (de Guzman, 2007, p. 3).

The first strategy to help teenagers is to nurture their abilities and self-confidence so that they could build positive friendships with other people. The ability of parents to strengthen family values could help a teenager to be firm in his or her decision to remain positive in all things. Second, teenagers must be encouraged to be close with caring adults. Caring adults like parents, teachers, guidance counselors, social workers, and relatives serve as a model for teenagers in matters of behavior and attitude. Third, parents should encourage their adolescents to create diverse relationships. The spiritual and sports activities sponsored by youth, church, and school organizations can provide a healthy and wholesome venue for competition, spiritual values orientation and skills development. Lastly, families with teenagers must be supported by governmental and non-governmental organizations in terms of parent education programs (de Guzman, 2007, p. 1). Support groups can provide information about negative effects of peer pressure found in books and publications, through seminar, open-forum, and regular meetings in a community (de Guzman, 2007, p. 1). By doing so, alcohol abuse and drug abuse due to peer pressure may be prevented.

C. Failure of Parents to Take Their Children Away From Harmful Activities

The role of parents in rearing their children is vital to their emotional, physical, psychological and mental development. Teenagers need the loving care and guidance of their parents in order to become successful in life. Besides, being free from harmful activities and safe from physical destruction must be the primary goals of parents for their teenage children.

Some untold problems are related to the role of parents in taking their children way from harmful activities. First, parents failed to teach their children about the negative effects of alcoholic beverages and drugs. Second, parents are the same persons who influence their children to drink alcohol and use drugs. And third, some parents neglect the basic needs of their children like parental love, care, attention, and financial support.

Basically, parents must teach their teenage children that any form of alcohol is harmful to the body. Being under the influence of alcohol weakens a teenager's judgment and self-control which could lead to violence, trauma and other form of abuse (Ballard, 2003, p. 58). Drinking alcoholic beverages can lead to alcoholism, which destroys individuals and families (Ballard, 2003, p. 58). On the other hand, any drug or chemical or dangerous practice that is used to produce a sensation or high can destroy a teenager's mental, physical and spiritual well-being. Parents must also develop a good communication pattern with their teenagers so that teachings and guidance for them can be properly given. Studies prove that parents who are more inclined to personally teach and guide their teenagers are more ensured of a happy and fulfilling parenthood (Ballard, 2003, p. 59). Therefore, failure of parents to take their children away from harmful activities affects teenagers and their future.

Another aspect of the problem is the choice of parents to influence their teenagers by means to drinking alcoholic beverages and using drugs at home and in other places with the presence of their loved ones. If a parent does not drink or use drugs, there is a huge possibility that children will follow the example. In other words, the behavior of parents still matter when it comes to delinquent attitudes of their children (Parents Who Drink Influence Their Teens to Do the Same Thing). In addition, contemporary research finding states that the example of parents and teachings are more effective forms of drug education compared to anti-drug programs in a community (Parents Who Drink Influence Their Teens to Do the Same Thing).

Parents need to consider these four points in keeping their children safe from alcohol abuse and drug abuse. First, environmental factors count more than genetics in terms of analyzing causes of alcohol abuse and drug abuse. Teenagers who live in an environment wherein using drugs and drinking is common are mostly the ones doing the same thing. Second, teenage children of heavy drinkers and drug addicts are heavily influenced by their parent's choices. And third, adolescence is a critical period for parents not to drink alcoholic beverages or use drugs. Parental habits and attitudes like

drinking alcohol and abusing drugs may influence teenagers. Hence, parents must refrain from heavy drinking and use of drugs especially in the presence of their teenage children.

Lastly, parents must not neglect their duty and obligation to provide adequate love, care, protection, guidance and financial needs to their teenagers. Teenagers who did not receive proper care and adequate attention from their parents will try to find it elsewhere. The worst scenario is when a teenager hangs out with friends who are drug addicts and heavy drinkers due to failure of parents to give physical, emotional, and financial support. The love and care a parent could give to a teenager may prevent their children from abusing drugs and alcohol. To this effect, parents must make their home a safe haven for their teenage children. Teenagers must not consider their homes as prison cells wherein parents are not practicing proper parental skills. There is no way to prevent teenagers from abusing drugs and alcohol except making their homes a place of love, kindness, understanding, and respect.

III. Possible Effects of Drug Abuse and Alcohol Abuse to Teenagers

The two well-known destructive effects of drug abuse and alcohol abuse among teenagers are sexual abuse and molestation as well as teenage pregnancy. Hence, we must analyze the problem to determine effective solutions.

A. Sexual Abuse or Molestation Against Teenagers

Going straight to the point, drinking alcoholic beverages and using drugs can cause inability of a teenager to use right judgment amidst a very uncompromising situation. Thus, teenagers must maintain proper behavior while socializing with other people. Since sexual abuse may be committed by a family member, dating partner, a friend, and even a teacher and caregiver, teenagers must refrain from drinking with these people and using drugs upon their request if any suspicious behavior and motives can be detected. For instance, a teacher who socializes with students must be reported to the police if a teenager finds her teacher asking for sexual favors in exchange of good grades. The more severe form of destruction against teenagers who are using drugs and alcohol is physical and sexual abuse which makes them develop a sense of

powerlessness and dependency leading to delinquency and adult criminality (Regoli & Hewitt, 2000, p. 191).

The most common causes of sexual abuse and molestation are alcohol use, drug abuse, risky sexual behaviors and having several dating partners (Hendrickson, 2001, p. 2). The use of drugs like cocaine increases the risk of sexual abuse between dating partners resulting to dating violence. It is the responsibility of parents to guide their teenagers in order to avoid the risks and causes of sexual abuse or molestation. Reports of medical experts stated that teenagers who have been sexually-molested are at advanced possibility for other health problems (Hendrickson, 2001, p. 2). Hence, treatment and monitoring are necessary if ever the problem occurred already.

B. Teenage Pregnancy

The usual causes of teen pregnancy are drug abuse and alcohol abuse while socializing with friends and dating partner (Henderson, 2008, p. 1). In fact, early use of drugs and involvement of heavy drinking increase the future risk of addiction, teenage pregnancy, and even infections of sexually-transmitted diseases. The direct cause of teenage pregnancy is drug and alcohol abuse because teenagers loose their ability to control themselves in sexual activities. For this reason, the basic idea is that drugs are not good for teenagers and not the other way around.

Teenage pregnancy poses great dangers to the child and the mother itself. Teenage mothers are three times more likely than other teenagers to stop going to school resulting to fewer earnings upon working. Teenage mothers are also likely to spend longer time of living in poverty compared to others. The worst problem related to teenage pregnancy is absence of husband. Raising a child without a husband is very challenging. Hence, most teenage mothers are likely to have delinquent child in a community.

Aside from that, children in poor, single-parent families, particularly those headed by teenage mothers, usually face peculiar trials and difficulties. They are more likely to practice chronic psychological distress, to participate in health-compromising behaviors such as drug and alcohol use, cigarette smoking, and unprotected sexual activities (Regoli & Hewitt, 2000, p. 178). Besides, these children are more likely to perform less in academic programs, to be suspended and even expelled in school, suffer from mental illness, commit suicide, and start their own single-parent families (Regoli

& Hewitt, 2000, p.178). Therefore, teenage pregnancy due to drug and alcohol abuse could cause destruction to the mother and her child.

C. Commission of Crimes Against Other People

Drug use and alcohol dependence can lead to teenage delinquency. There is a causal link between drug use and delinquency of a teenager (Regoli & Hewitt, 2000, p. 274). In addition, the use of alcohol is apparently associated with crimes of violence and sexual molestation (Regoli & Hewitt, 2000, p. 274). Research studies reported that between 40 and 80 percent of convicted murderers were under the influence of alcohol at the time of the commission of the crime (Regoli & Hewitt, 2000, p. 274). Aside from that, violent and heinous crimes are committed by people acting under the influence of drugs other than alcohol. A report from the National Institute of Justice Drug Use Forecasting mentioned that 26% of inmates in federal prisons and 29% of inmates in state prisons reported being under the influence of drugs at the time of their brutal offense.

Moreover, government reports also suggested that the more involved teenagers become in drug use and the drug business, the more likely they are to become implicated in the street addict lifestyle (Regoli, 2000, p. 275). Those teenagers most occupied in the crack distribution business and street addict lifestyle are also intensely implicated in violent crimes such as robbery, territorial disputes, and conflicts over money. Thus, it is confirmed that there is an association between drug abuse and alcohol dependency of teenagers with the commission of violent crimes.

The commission of violent cries due to drug and alcohol abuse often led to incarceration under the law. Teenagers who are convicted of crimes are forced to dwell in prison cells and correctional facilities with uncompromising situations to deal with. Most teenage male and female inmates tried escaping from jail in order to gain freedom from being imprisoned. Teenage girls who effectively run away often find themselves incapable to enroll in school or to acquire practical jobs and then be strained into the streets, where their survival may depend on petty crimes such as theft, panhandling, or prostitution.

IV. Drug Abuse and Alcohol Abuse: Solutions to the Problem

The need to help teenagers in relation to drug abuse and alcohol abuse problem makes it necessary to study the indispensable role of the government to provide venues

for its treatment and intervention. The concept of social justice is related to the problem of drug and alcohol abuse because it is the promotion of the welfare of all people and the humanization of laws so that social and economic equilibrium in the society can be attained (⌐Social Justice⌐). In other words, social justice is the equalization of social and economic forces for the benefit of the people. In this case, the social condition of teenagers who are victims of drug abuse, alcohol abuse, sexual abuse and molestation, and teenage pregnancy must be promoted by the professional who treats victims through effective intervention and treatment procedures.

The welfare of the youth is embossed within the policy-making power of the government. The evolution of social welfare programs for the youth happens slowly through the years (Ashton & Hull, 1999, p. 526). The government has established a systematic approach in helping teenagers achieve social justice. Thus, the presence of professionals emerges in the society with the support of the government. By professionals, we mean the individuals who are equipped with intellectual knowledge on the treatment and intervention for drug addicts and heavy drinkers.

The most common model used by professionals to treat drug addiction and heavy drinking includes generalist intervention model (Ashton & Hull, 1999, p. 526). Generalist intervention model is a practice model for professionals that offer step-by-step direction relating to the ways to undertake the planned changes process, which is generally aimed at addressing problems (Ashton & Hull, 1999, p. 526). The foundations of generalist practice are knowledge, skills, and values (Ashton & Hull, 1999, p. 32). With respect to knowledge, it means the strategies, models, and principles used in promoting the social condition of clients. Skills include the mastery to solve different problems of individuals and groups under difficult circumstances, and the ability in working harmoniously with other professionals that could help clients improve a better social condition. Values mean the use of ethical standards while working as a professional treating and helping clients who are victims of drug abuse and alcohol abuse.

V. Conclusion

The author affirmed that drug abuse and alcohol abuse is caused by stressful life events, peer pressure, and failure of parents to take their teenagers away from harmful activities. Adolescent drug use, then, is positively reinforced by contact to drug-using role models, endorsement of drug use by peers, and the apparent positive or pleasurable effects of the drug itself (Rigoli & Hewiit, 2000, p. 269). To conclude, it was proven in the research paper that indeed, the primary factors that influenced teenagers in using alcohol and drugs are friends and parents. Drug and alcohol abuse is also closely linked to the commission of violent crimes by teenagers such as murder, homicide and robbery.

Finally, effective parenting of teenagers may be the primary solution of drug abuse and alcohol abuse, but the effective intervention of professionals is indispensable when parenting teenagers fails (Dinkmeyer & McKay, 1990, p. 177). Therefore, there is no other way to intervene and treat teenagers with drug and alcohol abuse problems, but only through professionals who are willing to integrate all their knowledge, values, and skills in finding solutions to the same.

References

Aldworth, J. et. al. Division of Population Surveys, Office of Applied Studies. 2009. *Results from the 2007 National Survey.* Retrieved February 25, 2009, from http://www.oas.samhsa.gov/nsduh/2k7nsduh/2k7Results.cfm#2.2.

Ashman, K.& Hull, G. (1999). *Understanding Generalist Practice.* Chicago: Nelson-Hall Publishers.

Ballard, R. (2003). *Physical Health.* USA: Intellectual Reserve, Incorporated.

De Guzman, M. University of Nebraska Lincoln Extension, Institute of Agriculture and Natural Resources. *Friendships, Peer Influence, and Peer Pressure during the Teen Years.* Retrieved February 23, 2009, from http://www.ianrpubs.unl. edu/epublic/live/g1751/build/g1751.pdf.

Dew, Diane. Diane Dew Website. . 2009. *Teen Alcohol Abuse.* Retrieved February 27, 2009, from http://www.dianedew.com/drnkstat.htm.

Dinkmeyer, D. & McKay, G. (1990). *Parenting Teenagers.* Minnesota: American Guidance Service, Incorporated.

Drug Rehab Treatment Website. 2009. *Parents Who Drink Influence Their Teens to Do the Same Thing.* Retrieved February 23, 2009, from http://www.drugre habtreatmentcom/parental-influences.html.

Gunn, J. & Duncan, G. The Future of Children Website. 1997. *The Effects of Poverty on Children.* Retrieved February 23, 2009, from http://www.futureofchildren.org /usr_doc/vol7no2ART4.pdf.

Henderson, M. Times Online. 17 October 2008. *Drug Abuse a ⌐cause not effect⌐ of social problems.* Retrieved February 23, 2009, from http://www.timesonline. co.uk/tol/news/uk/science/article4958885.ece.

Hendrickson, G. Medicine Online. 30 September 2001. *Child Molestation-Child Sexual Abuse.* Retrieved February 23, 2009, from http://www.medicineonline.com /articles/c/2/Child-Molestation/Child-Sexual-Abuse.html.

Missouri Western State University. 2008. *Peer Influence on Deviant Behavior.* Retrieved February 18, 2009, from http://clearinghouse.missouriwestern.edu/manuscripts/ 853.asp.org/research/naswResearc/PublicHealth/default.asp>

Pasch, K. APHA Website. 17 November 2003. *Examining the processes of peer influence and peer selection and their relationship to adolescent alcohol use.*

Retrieved February 23, 2009, from

http://apha.confex.com/apha/131am/techprogram/

paper_65199.htm.

Regoli, R. & Hewitt, J. (2000). *Delinquency in Society.* USA: McGraw-Hill Companies,

Inc.

Sociology Guide. 2009. *Social Justice.* Retrieved February 23, 2009, from

http://www.sociologyguide.com/weaker-section-and-

minorities/SocialJustice.php.

Temke, M. University of New Hampshire Cooperative Extension. May 2006. *The*

Effects of Divorce on Children. Retrieved February 23, 2009, from

http://extension.unh.edu/Family/Documents/divorce.pdf.

Wattenberg, M. & Edwards, G. (2003). *Government in America: People, Politics, and*

Policy. USA: Addison-Wesley Educational Publishers Incorporated.

CPSIA information can be obtained
at www.ICGtesting.com
Printed in the USA
2712LVUK00001B